Beautiful by Design

Beautiful by Design

Stunning Blueprints for Harmonious Gardens

Tara Dillard

Sterling Publishing Co., Inc.

New York

Prolific Impressions Production Staff:

Editor in Chief: Mickey Baskett
Creative Director: Joel Tressler
Graphics/Photography: Joel Tressler
Illustrations: Shannon Pable
Administration: Jim Baskett

Library of Congress Cataloging-in-Publication Data

Dillard, Tara.
  Beautiful by design : stunning blueprints for harmonious gardens / Tara Dillard.
      p. cm.
  Includes index.
  ISBN 1-4027-1409-2
  1. Gardens--Designs and plans. 2. Landscape gardening. I. Title.
  SB473.D52 2004
  712'.6--dc22
                                                          2004009107

10 9 8 7 6 5 4 3 2 1

Published by Sterling Publishing Co., Inc.
387 Park Avenue South, New York, N.Y. 10016

© 2005 by Prolific Impressions, Inc.

Produced by Prolific Impressions, Inc.
160 South Candler St., Decatur, GA 30030

Distributed in Canada by Sterling Publishing
c/o Canadian Manda Group, One Atlantic Avenue, Suite 105
Toronto, Ontario, Canada M6K 3E7
Distributed in Great Britain by Chrysalis Books Group PLC,
The Chrysalis Building, Bramley Road, London W10 6SP, England
Distributed in Australia by Capricorn Link (Australia) Pty. Ltd.
P.O. Box 704, Windsor, NSW 2756 Australia

Printed in China
All rights reserved

For information about custom editions, special sales, premium and corporate purchases, please contact Sterling Special Sales Department at 800-805-5489 or specialsales@sterlingpub.com.

Sterling ISBN 1-4027-1409-2

Thank You, Margaret Moseley--Kelvin Echols and I were right to fight over you; Penny McHenry--what a dame; Walter Reeves and Gary Peiffer, my first and continuing promoters; Jenny Wolf, a tireless behind the scene garden doer.

Dana McPhearson & Bill Brown of Little Dixter, Virginia & her dog Miss Ellie Hendrick--you did it; Harriet Kirkpatrick--your garden is a tale; Lyndy Broder, Karen Klare, of the best French garden; Terri Rooks & Jo Anne Hall; Shirley Cole--a garden force; Rosemary & Nick Trigony, Phyllis & Tom Reetz--your garden is a multi-roomed gem; Kelley Dillard, Joel & Ellen Tressler, Lisa & Greg Shortell, Julie & Ric Ford, Gina & Mark Hill, Melanie & Richard Newton, Anne & Andy Sheldon--a beautiful garden for all the senses; Celine & Wade Stribling, Don & Kay Connelly--incredible self-taught gardeners; Sarah & Matt Miller, Kathy & Tom Trocheck, Audrey Newsome, Diane & Randy Mahaffey, Shannon Pable, Alice Williams, Paula Refi--a wonder with perennials; Jane Bath whom I'm proud to copy; Debbie Efird who is living a beautiful life.

Anna Davis--you have created a heaven here; Emily Pritchett, queen of the big castle garden; Renee & Denny Hopf, with a garden of serenity; Arch Baker--you put my garden in perspective.

If my first garden mentors were still alive they would be well over 100 years old. In memory of Louise Cofer whose garden awakened me; my gardening grandmothers, Bliss Page & Laura Sayers; and Mary Kistner whose eyes taught me to see.

COMMONLY USED TERMS

AXES - Views along a line in a garden.

DOUBLE AXES - As used by Tara Dillard - a single line with a focal point at each end.

ENFILADE - A view through to a view.

EVERGREEN - Plants that remain green all year.

FENG SHUI - Chinese art of placement.

FOCAL POINT - A bought object like a statue, or a stunning plant like a maple tree in fall.

PLINTH - A base to set something on.

SUBSIDIARY FOCAL POINT - Discreet focal point, such as small stone rabbit, not competing with a main focal point.

TABLE OF CONTENTS

In the Beginning -
My Early Gardening

Nothing demonstrates the quote below better than my early gardening when my own thoughts and viewpoints limited my artistry. I was "into" plants, they were my inspiration, and plants were the only things I wanted in my garden. During my first year, focal points or garden art pieces were not allowed in my garden - they weren't plants. When winter came, it brought a big lesson - my plants were either deciduous, completely devoid of foliage, or herbaceous and not there at all. My beautiful garden--the result of time, labor, money--disappeared because I had not planned for the winter conditions. Now, decades after beginning to garden, I am still a young gardener hungry for knowledge.

As the next early years passed, like the pendulum, I swung to the opposite extreme. Garden ornaments came into my garden in grand quantities as I tried to achieve what I saw in coffee table garden books. As I overdid it, my garden became tacky.

Finally through experience I learned that "less is sometimes more." Enlightenment led me to use one focal point per area. After an afternoon spent removing excess focal points, my collection of plants and accents became, at last, a habitat of graceful beauty. I also learned that it is important to put your focal points at the right height and to use the right style--one that fits with both your garden and house.

Gardening insists on a tough character trait--patience. It also requires that you open your mind in striving for beauty in your garden design. I hadn't wanted to unlearn old ideas that were no longer useful. But the unlearning of old ideas about your garden is as important as learning new ideas.

If your garden is young, it will probably be at least year three before you can exult, "Wow, my garden is finally here." My own "wow" moment came at year four when the resources of nature created what had been until then only hard work of my body and imagination. Patience paid off!

Decades have passed since I began gardening. I am still learning new ideas about simplifying a garden design. If forced to list the three top garden design rules, I would put them in this order: simplify, simplify, simplify.

> "to improve one's style means to improve one's thoughts and nothing else; he who does not admit this immediately will never be convinced of it."
>
> Nietzche

What I Learned from My Garden...

1. Gardens require patience. A garden doesn't happen overnight.

2. Striving for beauty in the garden is part of garden design.

3. Less can be more. Sometimes what is not there makes what is there more important.

4. My garden continually teaches me new ideas.

5. I had to unlearn old ideas that no longer served my garden. Gardens are everchanging--so should be your knowledge about your garden.

6. An important rule of garden design: Simplify.

7. The placement of focal points such as garden ornaments, garden art, or garden structures is one of the most important points of garden design. I had to learn what is the right style of ornamentation for my garden. I had to find the right place and right height for their placement.

8. Use one focal point per area. Simplicity is a virtue.

ABOVE: Subtle but still showy, this garden pot brings a three-dimensional element to a boring wall. The pot's plantings have a softening effect, as do vines growing elsewhere on the wall. Gertrude Jekyll, one of the world's first garden designers, said when she designs a garden the first thing she considers is what to put on the walls.

LEFT: A birdhouse home for the birds, with ivy making the birdhouse at home. I call this the rule of "just let it touch." Inorganic focal points look better with foliage just touching their edges. See chapter entitled, "Combining the Organic & Inorganic for Garden Art."

Elements of Garden Design

> *Your garden, like your attitude,*
>
> *is what you make of it.*

Designing a garden is much more than putting in plants. I learned that a garden needs structure--framework. I learned that a garden is not just about flowers. Once your structure is in place, then the luxury of choosing and planting flowers can begin. Through years of trial and error, and becoming attuned to what gives a garden beauty and grace, I have arrived at a formula for my style of garden design. Include these four elements in your garden and you will have created a framework that can give you 12 months of beauty.

1) turf or paths +
2) trees +
3) evergreen shrubs +
4) focal points

In the chapters of this book, I will concentrate on one of these key elements--focal points. I feel strongly enough about focal points to include them in every garden I design. Gardens designed without the structure of paths, trees, evergreens and focal points will be bare in winter. Early on in my garden design career, I certainly worked diligently at choosing and placing plants. But my gardens were only beautiful during the flowering season. If that same time, labor, and money had been put into some evergreens, garden structure, and focal points, I would have had plenty of beauty in my winter garden. Today, an important aspect of my garden design includes the use of focal points--their beauty is there year round.

You can achieve garden grace if you follow what has been done for centuries as classic garden design. Recapitulate the classic design, then add quirky exceptions to make it your own. Grace in your garden isn't just yours; it belongs to all that walk or fly its paths. When a garden acquires grace, you will finally cross the threshold of receiving more energy from it than you give to it.

What is a Focal Point?

A focal point is an object, usually other than a plant, that accents your garden. (An unusual or showy plant can also sometimes be a focal point or a temporary focal point--before it loses its blooms, for instance. An example of a plant focal point could be the winter tracery of a contorted filbert, Corullus Avellana, tree.) Common non-plant focal points are garden statuary or other garden art, garden structures such as benches, and practical items such as birdfeeders. My guidance about focal points within this chapter most often relate to the non-plant variety of focal point.

Focal points show a visitor which way to walk in a garden. Focal points catch your eye and call you to them. Focal points can be hidden surprises, only seen from certain areas in the garden.

How to Recognize a Focal Point

It is with focal points that you can make your garden uniquely yours. It is with focal points that your creativity can have a full workout. Many wonderful focal points weren't designed and made with gardens in mind, but an artistic eye can see them as the perfect accent for a particular spot in your garden. Think of an old wooden wheelbarrow holding pots of plants, for instance, as a garden focal point. Recognizing garden focal points in found items that originally had another purpose can become a whole creative hobby.

I do have a rule for purchasing focal points. Ask yourself, "Is this focal point so wonderful it will be fought

ABOVE: Yes, the blue/white porcelain balls are focal points, but more importantly, they are low maintenance. These pots will never need to be planted again. Ivy on the wall provides lushness the pots are lacking.

over at my estate sale?" If the answer is "Yes," then buy that item. Walk through your garden with that same question in mind concerning the ornamentation you currently have in your garden. All garden rules are breakable, but this one seldom is. Breaking this rule can result in a garden that I call "tacky." However, over many international garden travels, I have seen one garden that successfully used cheap, tacky focal points that no estate sale would want. It was an alluring, peppy, colorful little garden in Savannah, GA. I finally decided that it must belong to a voodoo princess, as it must have been voodoo to get me to like the cheap and tacky focal points.

Ideas for Beautiful Focal Points:
Garden Benches
Garden Furniture
Birdbaths
Birdfeeders
Birdhouses
Large unique planters
Gazing balls
Statuary
Arbors
Pots
Antique garden tools

ABOVE: Crash landing or focal point? Let loose with your wit and add interest. LEFT: Focal points in waiting. How exciting to find something like this fire grate for your garden especially if you don't know where or how it will be used. Anticipation. Life is good when you have focal points waiting in the wings to be used.

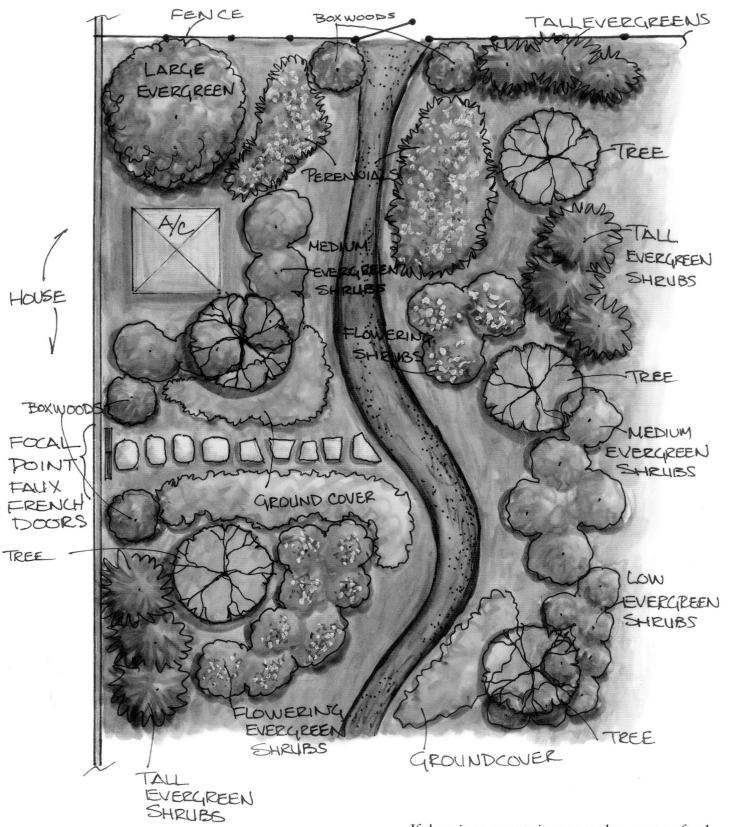

FENCE   BOXWOODS   TALL EVERGREENS

LARGE EVERGREEN

PERENNIALS

TREE

A/C

HOUSE

MEDIUM EVERGREEN SHRUBS

TALL EVERGREEN SHRUBS

FLOWERING SHRUBS

TREE

BOXWOODS

FOCAL POINT FAUX FRENCH DOORS

MEDIUM EVERGREEN SHRUBS

GROUND COVER

TREE

LOW EVERGREEN SHRUBS

FLOWERING EVERGREEN SHRUBS

GROUNDCOVER

TREE

TALL EVERGREEN SHRUBS

This Garden Plan Exhibits the Four Key Elements of Garden Design:

1. Paths
2. Trees
3. Shrubs
4. Focal Points

If there is an eyesore in your garden, create a focal point nearby to draw the eye away from the eyesore. Most homes have a side dominated by the air-conditioner. Don't leave that as the focal point. A path gently curves along the side of the house illustrated here, passing an air-conditioner that is cloaked in evergreens. The eye is drawn to a small side path of flagstones leading to a faux entryway, drawing attention away from the air-conditioner.

Elements of Garden Design...

1. Begin your garden design with turf/paths + trees + evergreen shrubs + focal points.

2. Spend your first efforts on what will be seen in your garden all year.

3. A garden of only deciduous and herbaceous plants will disappear in winter.

4. Recapitulate classic garden design. It's new every time.

5. Make focal points an important part of your garden design.

6. A focal point can be found or bought objects.

7. When buying a focal point, ask yourself, "Is this so wonderful it will be fought over at my estate sale?"

8. A temporary focal point can also be a plant, like a maple tree in fall.

9. Include your quirky passions as exceptions to garden design rules.

10. Keep focal point items in a garden to a few classic and top quality ones.

11. Keep focal point items in a garden open to the interpretation of whoever views them, especially yourself.

The Queen's Pot

If a garden is interesting it is also influential.

It was on a trip to Glamis Castle, Scotland that I had my favorite focal point epiphany, one I call "The Queen's Pot" epiphany. After touring crowded castle grounds it was time to follow the trail and get back to the bus. Far in the distance I saw a small meadow and intriguing woodland. After a few more steps, The Pot came into view. It was large, ancient, on a plinth, and empty. The meadow was mown with a lower strip--a path leading by the pot and into the woodland. A meadow, a path, a pot, and a woodland; gardens are such adult fairytales. That pot was singing to me like Bali Ha'i, and I was on my way. Up close, the pot and plinth were almost five feet tall. The woodland was an arboretum with trees over a century old and each one was labeled. A stream ran along the far edge and not another soul had ventured into "my" woodland. It was a pot so wonderful it said to me "yes, come this way," a pot so wonderful it was beautiful even when empty.

What is the Queen's Pot? It is the most beautiful pot you can find to be the focal point in an area of your garden. It is placed at just the right spot in your garden. It is exactly the right proportion for your garden. It is placed at exactly the right height. It holds all the riches of a beautiful garden. A garden should not be without a Queen's Pot.

Subsidiary focal points style a patio. The pictures on these two pages were taken in the garden of a couple who sail the globe extensively for work. These empty pots ("The Queens Pot" in miniature) are not only beautiful, they are reminders of various trips. The crystals, known for feng shui properties, were also collected on trips. Both the crystals and the vessels are low maintenance.

The Queen's Pot

was whispering,

"Come this way,

see my

lovely woods."

LEFT: Many good things about this plinth and pot may not be readily apparent. First, it was made by the gardener. He stacked stones and topped them with a stepping stone paver. Second, the pot is pretty enough to be a focal point without holding plants. Third, the pot can be emptied, turned over and used as a plinth for another pot, raising its height and increasing the drama.

My own "Queen's Pot" (drawing on opposite page) is set centered with the bay window of my living room. The placement is a perfect axis off the center of that room. As focal point it is a flower vase for both my interior and exterior views. Its placement took control of my front garden design. A formal herb garden, evergreen hedge, flagstone pathway and pairs of boxwood are all ancillary to the placement of my "Queen's Pot."

Design your focal point placement from your interior views of your garden. Many gardens, especially in subdivisions, let street views dictate design instead of the important views from the interior looking out into the garden. Be bohemian, don't care what the neighbors are thinking of what you are doing in your garden. Experience proves that when your garden is designed to be beautiful from the inside looking out, that beauty travels in two directions--yours and the neighbors'.

BELOW: If you're serious about low maintenance, container plants can become inconvenient. The solution is to purchase such wonderful containers that they can remain empty and still be a focal point. The pots shown aren't large but they are focal points without plants.

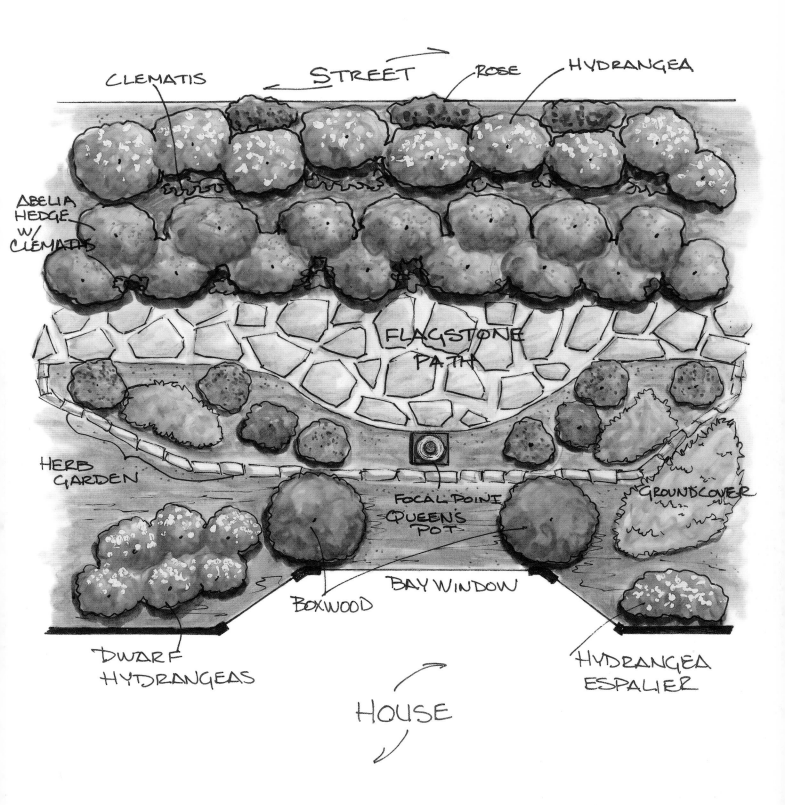

CLEMATIS

STREET

ROSE

HYDRANGEA

ABELIA
HEDGE
W/
CLEMATIS

FLAGSTONE
PATH

HERB
GARDEN

GROUNDCOVER

FOCAL POINT
QUEEN'S
POT

BOXWOOD

BAY WINDOW

DWARF
HYDRANGEAS

HYDRANGEA
ESPALIER

HOUSE

This plan shows "The Queen's Pot" seen through a bay window. This garden is intimate with the room it faces. Its focal point is a focal point for both outside and inside. Gardens and houses should be intimate with each other. Nurture your garden and it will nurture you.

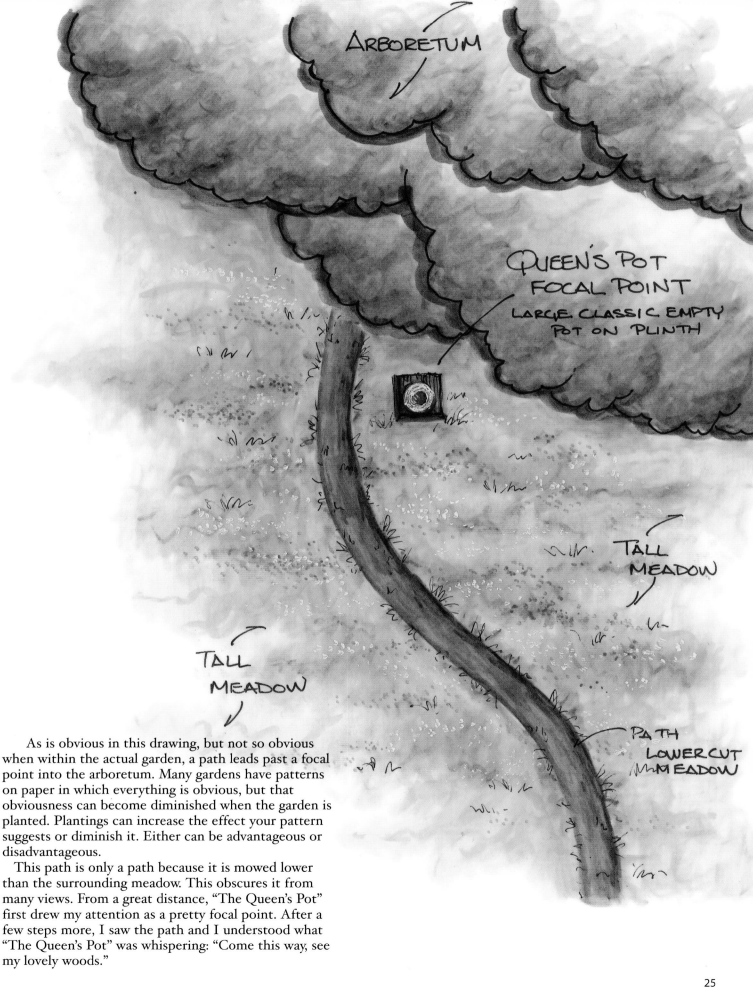

ARBORETUM

QUEEN'S POT
FOCAL POINT
LARGE CLASSIC EMPTY
POT ON PLINTH

TALL
MEADOW

TALL
MEADOW

PATH
LOWER CUT
MEADOW

As is obvious in this drawing, but not so obvious when within the actual garden, a path leads past a focal point into the arboretum. Many gardens have patterns on paper in which everything is obvious, but that obviousness can become diminished when the garden is planted. Plantings can increase the effect your pattern suggests or diminish it. Either can be advantageous or disadvantageous.

This path is only a path because it is mowed lower than the surrounding meadow. This obscures it from many views. From a great distance, "The Queen's Pot" first drew my attention as a pretty focal point. After a few steps more, I saw the path and I understood what "The Queen's Pot" was whispering: "Come this way, see my lovely woods."

The Queen's Pot...

1. Choose the most beautiful pot you can find to be a focal point.

2. The Queen's Pot is a beautiful pot, even when empty.

3. The Queen's Pot should be displayed at the proper height, on a plinth if needed.

4. Pots such as "The Queen's Pot" are low maintenance.

5. Your "Queen's Pot" should sing like Bali Ha'i.

6. Be bohemian, don't care what the neighbors think of your garden.

7. A "Queen's Pot" is a lure. Where are you luring garden visitors?...to a place, to an emotion?

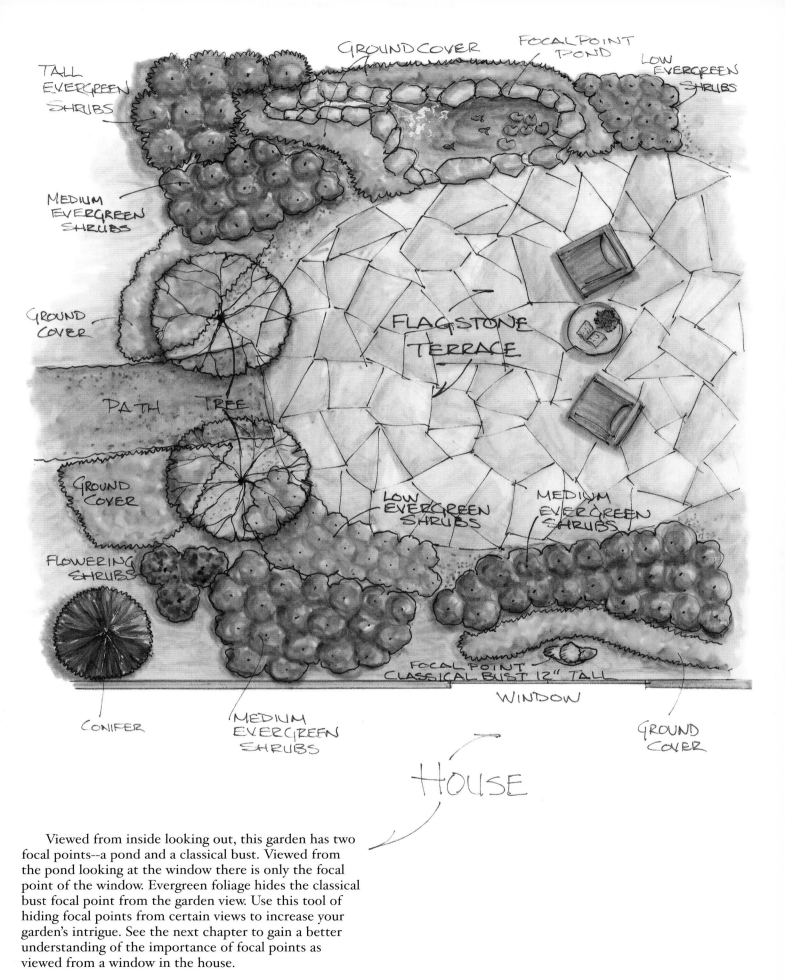

TALL EVERGREEN SHRUBS

GROUND COVER

FOCAL POINT POND

LOW EVERGREEN SHRUBS

MEDIUM EVERGREEN SHRUBS

GROUND COVER

FLAGSTONE TERRACE

PATH   TREE

GROUND COVER

MEDIUM EVERGREEN SHRUBS

LOW EVERGREEN SHRUBS

FLOWERING SHRUBS

FOCAL POINT CLASSICAL BUST 12" TALL

WINDOW

GROUND COVER

CONIFER

MEDIUM EVERGREEN SHRUBS

HOUSE

Viewed from inside looking out, this garden has two focal points--a pond and a classical bust. Viewed from the pond looking at the window there is only the focal point of the window. Evergreen foliage hides the classical bust focal point from the garden view. Use this tool of hiding focal points from certain views to increase your garden's intrigue. See the next chapter to gain a better understanding of the importance of focal points as viewed from a window in the house.

Where Should You Place a Focal Point?

Always leave space for birds and wind to plant in your garden.

Where should you place focal points? Begin inside your home by looking out your most common views-- from the kitchen, living room, and bedroom in most cases. Along those lines (called axes) place a focal point. Why put a bench or birdfeeder where you will never see them from the house? Make it a goal to have beautiful views from every window of your home. The beauty those views provide are worth the effort.

For each area of your garden, apply the rule: one focal point per area. You may discover this rule should be broken in some areas. If you have lots of focal points, are determined to use them all but the garden is telling you, "This is ridiculous, you're overdressing me," rotate your focal points display like a museum, replacing one with another periodically. A garden reinvents itself daily. Why can't we have personal reinventions as effortlessly as the garden seems to?

DRAWING OPPOSITE: When deciding where to place your focal points, stand inside your home and look out the most common views. Where the eyes go should be your genesis of placing a focal point. Create your own garden view. This front door has a garden bench with plantings for a focal point. It is much better than a typical subdivision home where you look out onto your neighbor's property. Determine to look out of your home and see your own focal points, not the neighbor's garage.

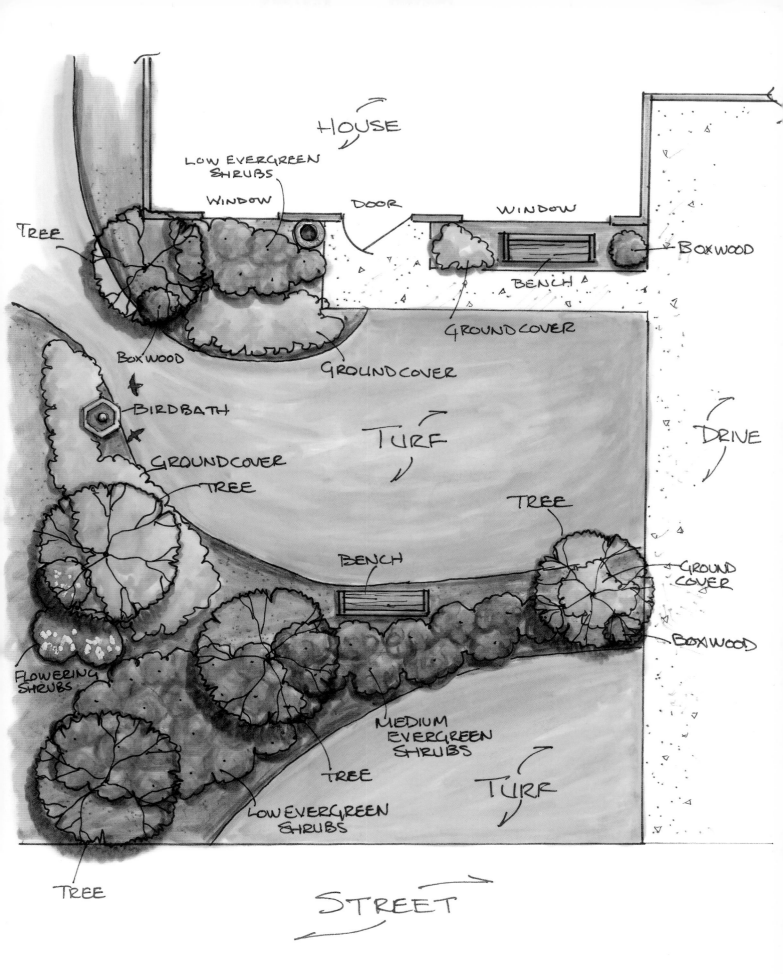

HOUSE

LOW EVERGREEN SHRUBS

WINDOW

DOOR

WINDOW

TREE

BOXWOOD

BENCH

BOXWOOD

GROUND COVER

GROUNDCOVER

BIRDBATH

GROUNDCOVER

TREE

TURF

DRIVE

TREE

GROUND COVER

BENCH

BOXWOOD

FLOWERING SHRUBS

MEDIUM EVERGREEN SHRUBS

TREE

TURF

LOW EVERGREEN SHRUBS

TREE

STREET

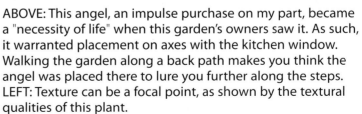

ABOVE: This angel, an impulse purchase on my part, became a "necessity of life" when this garden's owners saw it. As such, it warranted placement on axes with the kitchen window. Walking the garden along a back path makes you think the angel was placed there to lure you further along the steps.
LEFT: Texture can be a focal point, as shown by the textural qualities of this plant.

ABOVE: This fence is at the back of a garden, an area most gardeners overlook. Not this gardener. She saw a photograph in a magazine with old tools on a barn wall and copied the idea on her back fence. Not content with just the tools, she also styled the area with a pretty watering can. Because of the color of the tools, rubbed with boiled linseed oil for protection, they are a subsidiary focal point and not a main focal point.

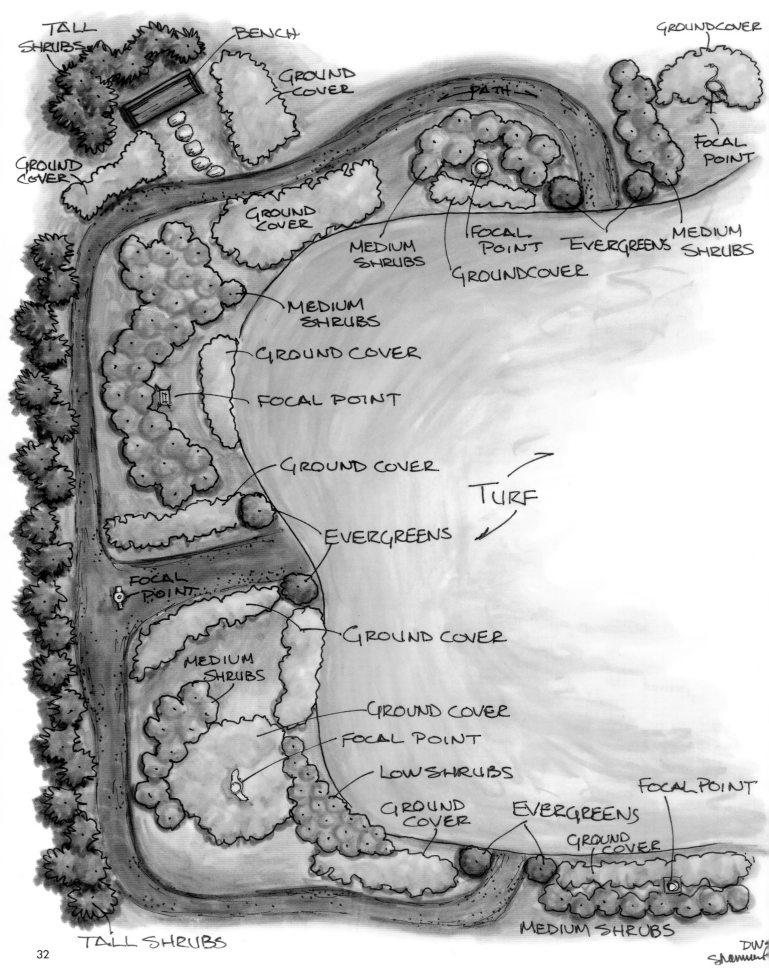

TALL SHRUBS

BENCH

GROUND COVER

GROUNDCOVER

GROUND COVER

PATH

FOCAL POINT

GROUND COVER

MEDIUM SHRUBS

FOCAL POINT

EVERGREENS

MEDIUM SHRUBS

GROUNDCOVER

MEDIUM SHRUBS

GROUND COVER

FOCAL POINT

GROUND COVER

TURF

EVERGREENS

FOCAL POINT

GROUND COVER

MEDIUM SHRUBS

GROUND COVER

FOCAL POINT

LOW SHRUBS

GROUND COVER

EVERGREENS

FOCAL POINT

GROUND COVER

TALL SHRUBS

MEDIUM SHRUBS

32

Where Should You Place Focal Points?

1. Place focal points on an axis with key views from inside your home.

2. Why place a birdfeeder where you won't see it?

3. Design focal point placement for you, not the neighbors.

4. Designing well-placed focal points is an act of grace.

5. Use one focal point per area. This rule can be broken, but only with much thought.

6. No room for all your focal points? Rotate them to suit your schedule.

7. Gardens change and you change. Make changes to refine your garden, as the spirit moves you to.

8. Entryways are always a focal point but are not counted in the rule of one focal point per area.

DRAWING OPPOSITE: This design includes ten focal points--seven hardscape and three organic. Entryways are always focal points; this garden has three. As an exception to the rule of one focal point per area, entryways in multiples are acceptable. With young plantings, this garden would be overwhelmed by its hardscape focal points--all would be visible at once. Mature plantings will caress the hardscape focal points into being focal points only in their separate garden areas, hiding them from each other.

A Window's Garden View

My garden

designs the

very air and light

around and in

my house.

When a garden is viewed from a window, it is as if the view is artwork on the wall, and the window is the frame. This takes you a step further in considering where to place your focal points. The view from your window is for you to enjoy and is so important that you must consider the placement of your art and garden furniture in relation to how they are viewed from your windows. Henry Francis du Pont thought so much of his window views at his famous home and garden (now a museum, Winterthur, outside Philadelphia, Pennsylvania) that he had four sets of window treatments made for his windows, one for each season. These draperies became the frames that enhanced his garden view--making his view art that changed with the season.

RIGHT: Looking through the panes of this door is like looking at a painting of a garden. Better than a painting, this gardener has changes of season with her window-- artwork. Why have focal points off your window views that are unattractive? Life is too short not to surround yourself with beauty and the strength it imparts.

Diminish eyesores by designing a focal point nearby to draw the eye and provide a resting spot.

My first perception of a garden view from the interior of the home as being artwork on the wall was through a huge 1950's multi-paned window placed into the living room wall of a 1920's Tudor style home. That garden view stopped my feet and halted my speech. It was a garden view of energizing art, a view that would forever change how I thought about garden views through windows. Window views must have a focal point and it must be set as if in a painting. Better than paintings, though, gardens change through the seasons and throughout each day. Who knew that your garden can be considered changing art on the wall?

This goes a step further than classic garden design dictates. It was never mentioned in lectures or books while I was in college, nor have I heard it verbalized in any seminar I've attended in over 20 years. Why? I think the increased pace at which we now live and the amount of technology required to keep pace makes us realize even more how important a nurturing organic realm is to our mental, physical, and spiritual health.

My epiphany about garden views being artwork on the wall was inspired by the garden of a woman completely untrained and unschooled in garden design. She created her garden after nearly dying from Lupus and grabbing hold of life with a shovel in her hand.

LEFT: There are two stories of windows on this house and, unfortunately, also power lines. The view, minus the power lines, is beautiful. The owners knew to create a focal point to draw the eye to somewhere fabulous, away from the power lines.

37

A Window's Garden View...

1. A view of a garden from a window can appear as artwork on the wall.

2. Determine to have beautiful views from every window.

3. Henry Francis du Pont had four sets of window treatments for many of his windows. This was to enhance the garden views of each different season being seen as artwork on the wall.

4. A window's garden view must have the focal point placed as if it were in a painting.

5. Your windows' garden views bring a nurturing organic atmosphere into the house for mental, physical, and spiritual health.

ABOVE: This home, built just after WWI, was designed and built by a returning soldier to remind him of his days being cared for by a French family after being wounded. The current owners have lovingly maintained this home and created a French style garden for it.
RIGHT: The garden view of this French style home, from an upstairs bedroom, appears as artwork on the wall. Colette would only find her beloved cats and perhaps a few chickens missing from the French style garden.

Garden Styles

Your style is what you have chosen to surround yourself with, on a daily basis, to make you happy. These choices have great impact. Interrelate the architectural style of your home, the style of your interior design, and the style of your garden.

There are many historic garden styles after which you can pattern your garden. Most American gardens fall under the informal style; the gardens being dictated by the area available and by the wishes and whims of the home owner, rather than a hard and fast style plan. But with a little knowledge of styles and the elements of design, you can create a garden that you not only love, but that has a form and function that loosely coheres to acceptable garden styles.

A Formal Style Garden

Formal gardens are defined by form and symmetry. The walkways are straight, the plantings are controlled, and the four quadrants of a garden space most often all mirror one another. Geometric shapes are abundant-- square planting spaces, rounded or cone shaped shrub forms. These types of gardens are most often seen in historic or heritage type homes. It would not be out of place to place a formal "garden room" into your overall garden plan.

The plantings are most often concentrated on shrub forms and have a limited color palette. One or two colors are considered appropriate in a formal garden. Boxwood and yew topiaries are the principle types of shrubs found in this style of garden. Roses and lilies can also play a role in formal gardens.

Focal points and ornamentation most often consist of formal statuary, urns, classic pot styles, and stone work. A freestanding fountain in a traditional design is effective as a central focal point. A freestanding fountain needs twice as much space around it as its height. A formal garden

lends itself to this because of its symmetrical design.

The Cottage Garden

This is an informal style of garden that is characterized by a riot of color and plantings that seem almost chaotic. The garden should be filled with plantings. A cottage garden relies heavily on perennial flowers. This type of garden is at its best during blooming season. Old fashioned plants such as hollyhocks, lavender, delphiniums, and daisies have a home in this garden style. Romance is the key word here.

Focal points such as rustic arches, wooden garden benches, and lacy metal work fences are appropriate here. Because of the informality, focal points with a bit of whimsy would not be out of place.

Informal American Garden

Usually this type of garden is what most family homes have. It is governed by what land we have available and our wishes for how we want to make use of the space. Mixed borders and plantings of annuals, perennials, bulbs, vines, grasses, trees and shrubs are appropriate. The owner's likes and dislikes are what determine the types of plantings used.

Because this is a family garden with an "anything goes" type of style, the focal points can be just that-- anything goes. But with taste. Here is where a beautiful copper wind bell, or an antique wheelbarrow can feel at home. Particular themes can be carried out within this style. Mediterranean gardens with their vine covered pergolas, outdoor dining areas, herbal plantings, and a layed back, earthy style is a trend that is emerging. Walled gardens or courtyards are another theme that is popular today. They are intimate spaces that are perfect for relaxing and entertaining. Wild gardens with a certain

continued on page 42

ABOVE: Flowing lawn, clean lines, beautiful plantings, and good maintenance pay homage to the house as focal point in this back garden. Never underestimate the power of a simple good garden.
OPPOSITE: This is a view out from the house. Subsidiary focal points can be spotted but the main focal point is the garden. Creating gardens as focal points around your home is like having a buffer zone of serenity from the outside world. Another benefit of designing a beautiful garden will be all the birds attracted.

continued from page 40
amount of planned control are popular in today's environmentally conscience society.

Asian Influenced Gardens

These gardens have a carefully planned asymmetry. The placement of all the elements of the garden are done to achieve balance from any viewpoint. The garden's focus is on rocks, water, and evergreen plantings. Pebble walkways lead one through the garden. Bamboo structures, wooden elements, large boulders, art, and lanterns are the focal points of choice. Harmony is the feeling evoked in these gardens.

Design Factors

No matter the style of garden that is chosen, key elements of good design should always be considered.

- Color: The garden style you choose will determine whether you have one color of blooming flowers or all colors of the rainbow.

- Form: Shapes of plants and relation to their proximity to other plantings need to be considered.

- Texture: This goes hand in hand with form. Coarse, soft, feathery are some of the textures that need to be considered for maximum effect.

- Line: This element controls the eye movement within the garden space.

- Scale: Consider the size of one component in relation to an adjacent component. This should not only be considered in your plantings, but in the items you choose for your ornamentation and your focal points.

Let the Garden Decide

A small perennial border that I created, following proper design and soil preparation guidelines, went from its fall planting to its spring and summer debut more

ABOVE: Much is in this tiny space yet it looks simple. Colorful potager (vegetable garden), gravel path with stone edging, bench, plinths with ferns, and backdrop hedge--more seems less. Think through the years about this focal point. The bench can change color, the ferns can be replaced with bright annuals, plinths can be replaced with hydrangeas, or the potager can have green ground-cover instead of bright annuals. Slight changes can have a huge impact on this focal point--big impact with little input.

beautiful than any other garden room on my property. It was the first time I had let go of my will for the garden and let the will of my garden finally express itself entirely. Not only was this little garden beautiful, it was beautiful quick. I wanted a focal point in that garden, but the garden said, "Tacky girl, I don't need a focal point." Sometimes no focal point is the correct choice.

This little garden influenced other areas of my life. It stopped me one afternoon and said, "You choose the plants to put in your garden, choose the people to have in your life." Toxic people in my life suddenly disappeared thanks to that beautiful little garden. Had a focal point been there I believe it would have distracted me from hearing what I needed to hear from the garden.

A garden should not be

multiplied beyond what is needed.

ABOVE: Why not? It's been done many times. Imagine a French style chair, painted Monet green and blooming with overstuffed tulips. Oh dear, now I'm wanting a pair of those French chairs stuffed with tulips. If the chairs are mismatched I'll paint them the same color and shimmy one so they're both the same height.

Interior and Exterior Should Complement

If I kept a tally of my clients who have beautiful interior design and hideous exterior garden design, the percentage would be high. When most of us start gardening, our homes have a dual personality disorder. The interior personality is happy and well adjusted while the exterior personality is dysfunctional indeed. Get rid of the exterior dysfunction by looking to the architectural style of your home and its interior decoration.

A couple hired me to redesign the garden of their Tudor style home. Its garden was already nice in a traditional style. However, when I entered the home, I saw that it was completely done with oriental motifs. Then I knew why I had been hired. The history explained it. Their home, set in the English countryside, was that of a retired, eccentric Englishman returned from years of working in China. The garden, the architecture, and the interior now all tell the same story. Choosing the style of their focal points and plantings became easy.

Continued on page 47

ABOVE: Placed to the left of the front door this sitting area is very welcoming. It also works well with the Tudor style home. The gardener has found this to be an area she uses a lot. That's another benefit of good design--you will use your garden more for pleasure.

RIGHT: Big touches are done well in this entry garden. Magic is interjected with subsidiary focal points so subtle they aren't really noticed until you're on your way up the steps. Look closely, the first two steps have a collection of diminutive trough gardens.

There's a fine line between subsidiary focal points being magic or tragic. But follow through on your crazy ideas; nothing will force you to keep them if they work better in imagination than reality.

Continued from page 44
    Choosing a garden style that plays with the story of your interiors makes gardening easier and streamlines the selection of focal points. For a long while I was notorious for buying any focal point that was well priced and not tacky. It led to this rule: Do not buy a focal point just because you are there, it's passable, and the price is good. Just "passable" focal points will make your style statement lose impact or disappear. Determine to make your house and garden one, no separation.

LEFT: Outdoor dining tables are focal points. Make sure yours is functional for your needs and also pretty to look at from inside your house. A square or rectangular dining table is best for most patios. Two square tables can be separate or brought together. (Round tables waste a lot of space.)
    Go for classic styling and estate sale quality. If you get the right patio dining table, you won't buy another. Patio tables and their chairs don't have to match. A metal and glass table still looks classic with a set of wood chairs.

> *Gardens are about contracts in color, form, and texture.*

Whimsy is at Home in a Garden

Eclectic focal points such as a tall 1930's copper light fixture used as a trellis can have impact in a witty manner. It's always fun to use something in a new creative way. Wit can be a bosom friend choosing focal points, while "cute" usually kills by being trite and hackneyed. Pay attention to subtleties.

RIGHT: Here's perfect frisson. Gardens are about contrasts. Consider small leaves next to large leaves, burgundy foliage next to green foliage, round flowers next to spikey flowers. This woodland garden has a focal point straight from Greek mythology. If you don't know what to choose for a focal point, begin by thinking what would add contrast to the area.

New gardeners

talk flowers,

old gardeners

talk foliage.

Emotions play a Role in Garden Style

An interior design magazine, many years ago, wrote that we recreate the rooms that first impressed us at a young age. Yes, looking up at my home from that magazine, I did see a good copy of the first rooms that impressed me, and out my windows I saw garden rooms that were solid renditions of the first gardens to impress me.

Long Barn, the first garden that ever made a deep impression on me, at age 22, was in England and owned by Vita Sackville-West. I saw pictures of it in a book, The Flower and The Nettle, written by Anne Morrow Lindbergh about her life there just after the murder of her baby and subsequent trial of the perpetrator. Reading her description of a climbing rose rambling in a second story window and scenting the entire room made me cry. My life was nowhere near having scented roses growing into a room to find me.

Anne's book is a journal of her days, not a garden book. Yet it is a garden book. After rereading the book, I'm convinced the garden at Long Barn and its relationship with the house was a factor in Anne learning to live with her grief. I also spent much time studying the garden pictures she took. They taught me about keeping focal point items in a garden to a few, classic, top quality ones, open to the interpretation of whoever views them.

Likewise, I am emotionally supported by my garden. Whatever mood I'm in, my garden is there to work with it and help me move forward with grace and serenity.

Anne Morrow Lindbergh introduced me to Vita Sackville-West. Vita was leasing Long Barn because she had purchased Sissinghurst. Sissinghurst has become one of the worlds most visited gardens. What wonderful taste I had discovered. I had been so impressed by the garden at Long Barn years before I knew of Vita's accomplishments with Sissinghurst--the site and inspiration of many of my own garden epiphanies. (One of those epiphanies is: The more axes from which a focal point is viewed, the better the garden.)

Joseph Campbell, expert on mythology and spirituality, said that it's amazing in hindsight that our lives do have a clear plan. Our gardens often play a part in the plan.

OPPOSITE: Backlit by morning sun, the colorful pealing bark on this tree is a main focal point. More precious because of its tenuous existence. Moments later, without the sun, the bark is just another subsidiary focal point. Your garden may have a formal pond with large statue spraying water as its focal point but if a mature ornamental cherry tree is nearby in full bloom it's no contest as to which is the main focal point. Do add certain plants for momentary but overwhelming displays as focal points in your garden. Cover the months so you have at least one plant peaking each month with a final goal of having a different plant coming into peak every two weeks.

Real gardeners always say the same two things, "You should have seen my garden last week when the _____ was blooming," and "You should come see my garden next week when the _____ is in bloom."

ABOVE: This garden will have as many first impressions as the people who visit it--impressions like: Whoa, this is wonderful, a wonderland; Way too busy; Does the gardener maintain this without help?; Maybe I should rethink the paint colors on my house; I could move in tomorrow. Whether or not you like the house and garden, it is apparent the gardener must be an interesting person. From experience, I know that artistic gardens, created and maintained by an artistic owner, are not about making outward impressions. Instead, they are planted expressions of a joy and love for plants and aesthetics--a joy so enveloping they have combined house, garden, and life into a seamless whole. These are people that have realized they want their exterior life to match their interior life.

*Never underestimate
the power of a simple good garden.*

ABOVE: Small details add up to large impressions. This copper round gutter melds into the backdrop of home and garden. Typical rectangular white gutters are eyesores unless on a white backdrop. Imagine a white gutter and downspout in this picture instead of copper. Copper gutters aren't in every budget but white gutters can be affordably painted to blend in with their backdrop.

LEFT: Just let it touch. This face is a part of the garden because of the way she is caressed by foliage. Having coarse and fine textured foliage near adds lushness.

ABOVE: Small and off to the side, this focal point could be a reminder of a vacation to Italy.

RIGHT: Put an empty jug by those stone steps. That doesn't sound interesting but the line of this vessel lends an air of grace to these stone steps. Sometimes subsidiary focal points look good in practice though they seemed horrible in theory. That's another reason why gardening can absorb us for a lifetime--it will take at least that long to figure it out.

A Garden Style...

1. Architectural style, interior design, garden design, and focal point style should be interrelated.

2. Beautiful interior design with a horrendous garden has a name--dysfunctional.

3. Your architectural house style, interior design, garden design, and focal point style should all tell the same story.

4. We try to recreate the gardens that first impressed us in youth.

A Garden Style...

5. Do not buy a focal point just because you're there, it's "passable," and the price is good.

6. Boring focal points will make your whole garden boring.

7. Wit can be a bosom friend when choosing focal points.

8. "Cute" focal points can kill a garden by being trite and hackneyed.

9. The more axes from which a focal point is viewed, the better the garden.

ABOVE: On axis with the front door, this garden view is pretty in summer but becomes plain in winter. It's an instance of thinking "ooh, a missing focal point." You should mentally "garden" every garden you visit. Question, question, question. It hones your skills for your own garden.
LEFT: Too much but it's great. A frog swinging his legs on the edge of a birdbath planted with annuals, mulched with polished rocks, and proudly displaying a clear crystal ball that splinters the sun in the center. Well, if this isn't the beginning of a short story, what is? Created by an 87 year old gardener, I'm still stunned at the frivolity of this focal point. Most of us have a few decades to go before we become so young.

ABOVE & OPPOSITE: In the United States, before 9/11 garden photographers would commonly remove the American flag to get a more perfect shot. Tragedy has changed even minor details of our cultural anthropology. This front door is everything it should be: it is welcoming, crisply painted; it uses great hardware and interesting house numbers; it is lushly yet simply planted with emphasis on a pair of potted boxwoods; it's well maintained and a is great destination at the end of an old fashioned path.

Creating Your Garden Style

When choosing a garden style or theme, overdose on it. If your stucco house warrants a French theme, overdose on it: use paint color, door hardware, light fixtures, statuary, pots, lavender plants, patio furnishings, evergreen hedges fronting countless bulbs, hydrangeas, and anything else that says French to you.

Consider:
Lavender
Rosemary
Metal Ornamentation
Metal Fences
A wall fountain
Outdoor dining furniture
Parterres (a square or rectangular area that is
   subdivided into equal parts by intersecting
   paths)

A formal Italian villa theme would include low evergreen hedges backed with mostly evergreen flowering shrubs and at least one tall, thin cone shaped evergreen. Also use large terra cotta olive jars as focal points or a small grotto stuccoed with shells and quartz. Include a grape covered arbor over a flagstone terrace and long trestle table for al fresco meals.

Consider:
Boxwood hedges
Herbal gardens
Pergolas
Statuary
Terra cotta
Stone
Topiaries

Carefully planned garden rooms and focal points should align with interior rooms. Yes, overdose your theme to the maximum. But don't overdose with the quantity of focal points. Austerity can create intensity.

ABOVE: This hose guide is for function but its pattern makes it a subsidiary focal point. The pattern is repeated in other places in the garden: shutters, finials and containers. Repetition is a great tool of garden design.

"Love is best kept in separate gardens."

Kelley Dillard

Oriental, English cottage, Deco, mid-century modern, Moorish--there is a theme waiting for you to overdose with. In business school they would call this branding.

ABOVE: What are you going to do with a basement door? Make it a focal point. This gardener makes creating a basement door entry look easy. Elements to think of: plantings on the house, interesting door color, good hardware, appropriate light fixture, maybe a wall plaque, plain urn with a metal topiary.

You may not use your basement door often, but it is often a focal point while in your garden looking back at the house. Who cares that the basement isn't finished? If the entry is designed, people will think you have a wine cellar and home theater.

Serene gardens require waiting because much of their serenity comes from mature plantings.

RIGHT: Using plants as focal points creates serene gardens. Plants can be temporary focal points like this blooming hydrangea in summer or a bright colored maple in fall. Broad winding paths of turf are an element of many serene gardens. They carry the feet and eyes, but metaphorically they run like a river.

The illusion of work about to be done in a garden

is almost like looking at completed work.

OPPOSITE: When you're entertaining and the garden is a mess, it's easy to choose an exterior temporary "theme"--the gardener's work about to be done. Gather a few tools and style them as if for a photo shoot where your guests will see them. Never make a comment. Buy a flat of colorful annuals and place it near your front door with an old trowel. Place another flat just at the edge of the area your guests will see. Again, never make a comment--your guests will do it for you.

The illusion of work about to be done in a garden is almost like looking at completed work.

ABOVE: Use a collection as a focal point: trough collection, moss collection, plinth collection.

Creating a Garden Style...

1. Rule for your garden style: overdose on it.

2. Overdose your theme, but not the quantity of focal points.

3. Austerity can create intensity.

4. Oriental, English, French, Italian, Moorish--there is a theme waiting for you to overdose with.

5. Business schools would call overdosing a theme branding.

LEFT: Yes, you are seeing an unusual and functional focal point--a water fountain. This garden is in a neighborhood with sidewalks and where most neighbors know one another. It's a walking, riding, skating, jogging, stroller neighborhood. This gardener realized she could offer water to her neighbors while having some herself during all her gardening.

ABOVE: House numbers should always be easily seen and of a style matching the house. It is said we have less than six seconds to make an impression.

Color Counts

*Garden
and be well.*

Color itself can be a garden theme. It is also one of the key elements of design to consider when developing your garden style. Black or green are classic color themes in America. Shutters, front and back doors, pots, urns, patio furnishings, cushions, and statuary--all become part of your color scheme. It's a great idea and an old one. Alternating generations seem to discover the color theme idea, an idea that makes choice easier.

Color counts with focal points, too. New concrete statuary is easily affordable but most of it looks cheap, as well. While touring a small elegant townhouse garden with a prestigious address, I was in awe of the money spent in such a small space. However, the pride of place was a new concrete statue, not stone or cast stone. It was on perfect axes from several locations. But no effort had been made to age or amend the color. A handful of pond muck rubbed on and hosed off would have turned that

cheap glinty concrete statue into aged art instead of an aesthetic torpedo. That otherwise beautiful garden magnified the mistake of a focal point with terrible color.

OPPOSITE PAGE: Steps are always a focal point and these have been dressed with summer color. The granite steps were originally city curbstones.
ABOVE LEFT: Have fun choosing your seasonal annual color. Get a large cart at the nursery and start grabbing colors that appeal to you. Arrange them on the cart for color combinations; some will be rejected and the rest go home. Photograph your better color combinations to use as reference in future years.
ABOVE RIGHT: Color can be a focal point. These hot pink flowers make you look. This little birdbath began life as the bottom of an umbrella stand.

A handful of pond muck rubbed on and hosed off would have turned that cheap, glinty, concrete statue into aged art instead of an aesthetic torpedo.

If your patio furnishings are "field gathered"--meaning some from the store, some from garage sales, some from the side of the road-- paint them all the same color. (That is if they are all worth keeping. Patio furnishings, poorly chosen, are the number one ugly item I discover and tell clients to replace. No color can save them. Ugly is ugly.) Cushions on patio furniture are best made of a solid color that matches a major color of your interior design. Floral or striped cushions, especially if bought off the shelf, can destroy a garden. Why make a cushion the focal point? Floral pillows are best used as accent pillows and should ideally match a floral pattern from your interior.

RIGHT: Spring is joyfully heralded. Fall is the under-appreciated season. Colors of fall are intense and shocking. Burnt orange leaves may land around your still blooming antique pale pink roses. Pow, it gets our attention.

Add fall color to any garden design decisions you make up front. Fall color is a seasonal focal point. Place some of those trees you're choosing for fall color where their winter shadows will grace a wall of your home or slant across the lawn. It's a powerful feeling to design where shadows will be in winter.

The chair had no other function than to be pretty...

Investigating the walled garden of Sir Walter Scott taught me the value of a well-placed chair and color. Within the large space, in a corner, was a tiny bit of garden with these ingredients: gravel path, tall ancient stone wall, strip of turf, evergreen shrubs, herbaceous plants, and an old iron chair painted white. The chair had no other function than to be pretty in its setting...and it was. That chair is the genesis of my recommendation to purchase a pair of old iron chairs at an antique market or garage sale, paint them a shocking color pulled from your interior artwork, and place them about your garden. They're not to sit on, they're to look at from a distance. Their age will add uniqueness to your garden.

OPPOSITE PAGE: Gardens using differing shades of green as a color theme are serene gardens. A touch of gray foliage makes a green garden more intense.
TOP RIGHT: This mailbox brings the color of the house to the street. If your mailbox is on a wooden post paint it the color of your shutters or front door.
ABOVE LEFT: Not much can be done about the necessities on the roof of this house but the house colors draw attention away from those eyesores. It's an old house and the colors are historically accurate.

Exterior trim, shutters and front door can all be the same color or they can be three different colors.

Downspouts from your gutters are probably not on your radar, but put them there momentarily. Downspouts painted white, running against any other color, perform visually like columns. Paint downspouts the color of your bricks or siding. Copper gutters and downspouts are classic and need no painting.

Front doors should be a focal point. They can also be painted a different color than your shutters and trim. Black is thought of and accepted as elegant and rich looking, but my opinion is harsher. From a distance, a black front door recedes, looking like a dark hole. If the bricks or siding can handle it, paint your front door a color that shows up repeatedly in most of your interior artwork. If that color is just a bit out of your comfort

zone and works well with your home's exterior, you've found your new front door color.

Exterior trim, shutters, and front door can all be the same color or they can be three different colors.

ABOVE: These new bricks, left over from the Atlanta, GA Olympics, still need a significant amount of aging. Their color isn't at home yet in this old setting. Notice the old pierced brick wall in the background. To age new hardscapes faster, pour a mixture of buttermilk, moss, and cow manure over them.

OPPOSITE: Moss gardens are the magic carpets of any winter garden. Their winter color peaks into a changeable chartreuse.

Color Counts...

1. Color itself can be a theme. Pots, statuary, shutters, trim, and furnishings all work well when they are the same color.

2. Focal points of cheap concrete should be aged or stained.

3. Field gathered patio furnishings can all be painted the same color to unify them.

4. Patio cushions should not be striped or floral. Why make cushions a focal point?

5. Patio cushions should be a solid color chosen from inside the house.

6. Place an old, colorful iron chair in your garden for artistic accent.

7. Don't let your downspouts be "columns." Paint them the color of your siding rather than white or a light contrasting color.

8. Look at your interior artwork to choose a front door color.

OPPOSITE: Hydrangeas are always a favorite because they provide masses of color. Spike hydrangea color by companion-planting it with clematis. Hydrangeas are blue in acid soil, pink in alkaline soil.
   Keeping a garden low maintenance yet full of color is best done with flowering shrubs acclimated to your zone.

Enfilades

A garden doesn't say anything
it is merely a provocateur.

An enfilade is a view through to a view. Enfilades increase the impact of your focal points. They are also the design element that has propelled more gardens onto the covers of books and magazines than any other. Viewing a statue is fine. But compare it to viewing a statue through a pair of boxwoods, over a water fountain, through another pair of boxwoods and a walk with a flowering shrub border on each side. There at the end is the statue--perfection with drama.

DRAWING OPPOSITE: Once you discover how to create an enfilade, a view through to a view, your garden will not remain unchanged. This garden view takes your eyes through several pairs of trees and boxwoods and two garden rooms before finally landing at a bench. Look at old garden magazines you've saved and notice how many cover photographs are of garden enfilades.
ABOVE: This enfilade draws you down a path and past a pond to two rooms.

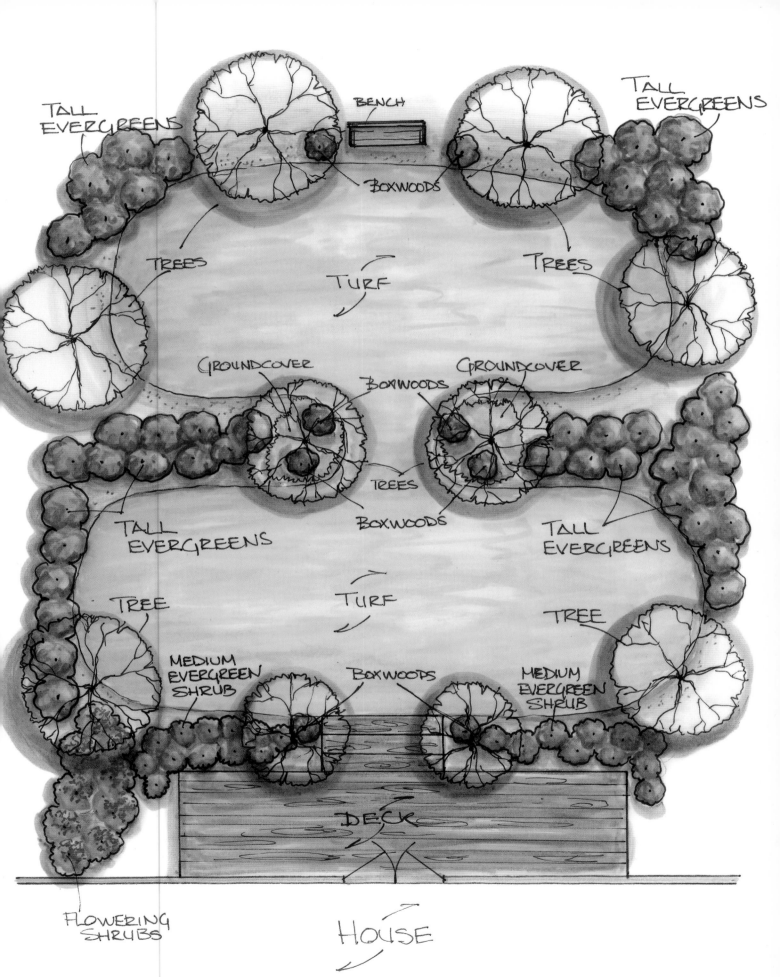

TALL
EVERGREENS

BENCH

TALL
EVERGREENS

BOXWOODS

TREES

TREES

TURF

GROUNDCOVER

GROUNDCOVER

BOXWOODS

TREES

BOXWOODS

TALL
EVERGREENS

TALL
EVERGREENS

TREE

TURF

TREE

MEDIUM
EVERGREEN
SHRUB

BOXWOODS

MEDIUM
EVERGREEN
SHRUB

DECK

FLOWERING
SHRUBS

HOUSE

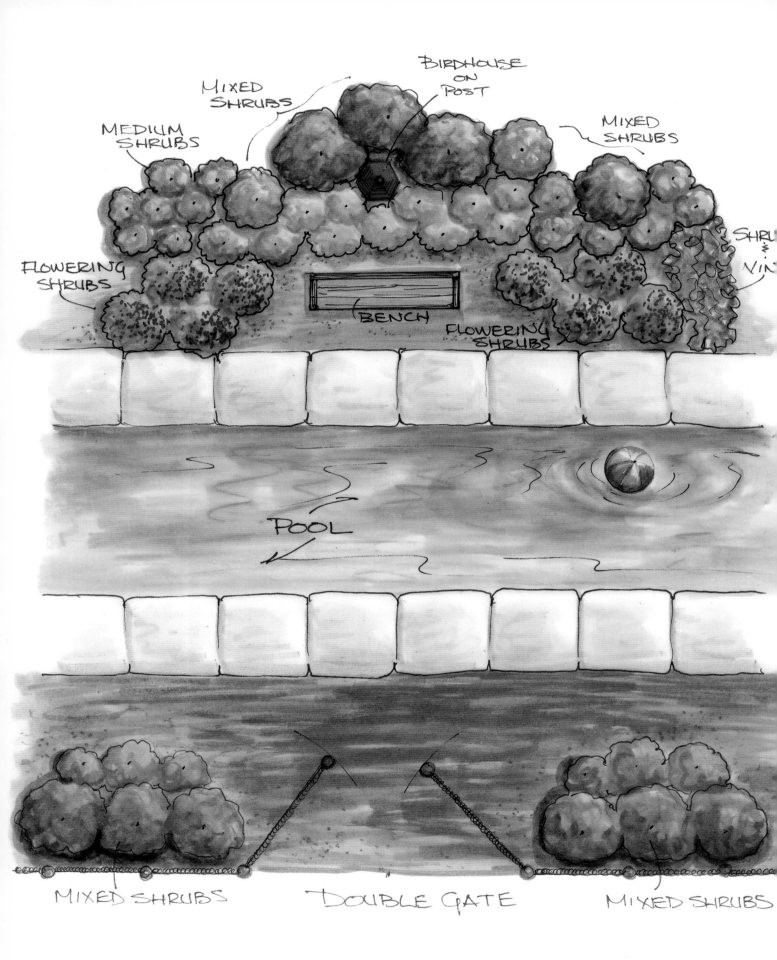

MIXED
SHRUBS

MEDIUM
SHRUBS

BIRDHOUSE
ON
POST

MIXED
SHRUBS

FLOWERING
SHRUBS

SHRU
VIN

BENCH

FLOWERING
SHRUBS

POOL

MIXED SHRUBS

DOUBLE GATE

MIXED SHRUBS

DRAWING OPPOSITE AND PICTURED ABOVE: Through a double gate, past stairs, across the pool, and landing at a beautifully planted bench, birdhouse and fence. Wow. Train yourself to think of gardens or pictures of gardens as a drawing. With enough thought you can recreate garden areas you love in your own garden. I like to think that "copying" is the second rule of garden design after "simplicity."

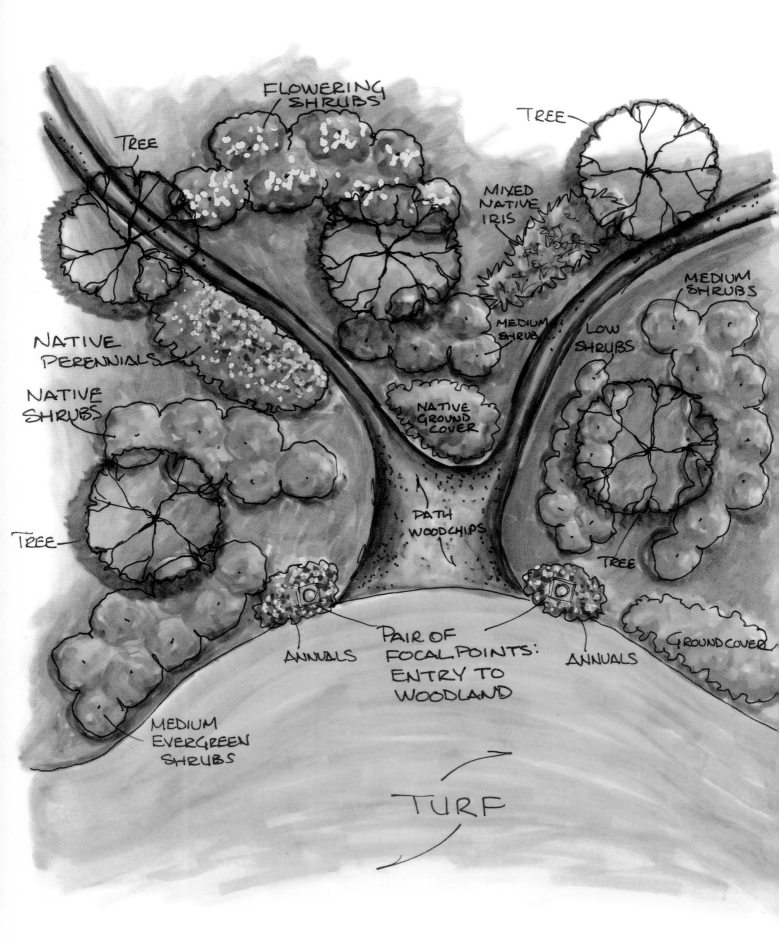

FLOWERING
SHRUBS

TREE

TREE

MIXED
NATIVE
IRIS

MEDIUM
SHRUBS

NATIVE
PERENNIALS

MEDIUM
SHRUB

LOW
SHRUBS

NATIVE
SHRUBS

NATIVE
GROUND
COVER

TREE

PATH
WOODCHIPS

TREE

ANNUALS

PAIR OF
FOCAL POINTS:
ENTRY TO
WOODLAND

ANNUALS

GROUND COVER

MEDIUM
EVERGREEN
SHRUBS

TURF

DRAWING OPPOSITE & PICTURED ABOVE: Enfilades are not just for formal gardens, they are also effective in informal woodland gardens. Whether formal or informal, focal point rules remain unchanged.

Enfilades

increase

the impact

of your

focal points.

A View Through to a View...

1. Enfilades increase the impact of your focal points.

2. An enfilade is an important design ingredient of the best gardens.

3. Enfilades are effective in both formal and informal gardens.

4. Enfilades help your eyes move through the garden.

RIGHT: Enfilades are views through to a view. Here the enfilade is through the arbor and past the pool to the statue. It's also on a double axes because there is another focal point opposite the statue (see below).

BELOW: You're looking at the same arbor but from the opposite direction from that shown above. When creating a focal point area, remember that another focal point area is automatically being created in its opposite direction.

Subsidiary Focal Points

Gardens are an escape. Gardens embrace life.

Subsidiary focal points are hidden surprises. They are smaller items, perhaps overlooked by visitors, like a stone rabbit tucked under a bush appearing to nibble foliage. Clusters of items, perhaps several trough gardens, can create a subsidiary focal point and add the air of a collector or connoisseur. A formal herb garden with Pan as its focal point was already pretty to me when I discovered, under the foliage and hips of a nearby climbing rose, a life-sized carved wooden black crow. He had attitude and he did surprise me. Subsidiary focal points should be discreet and not compete with the main focal point.

ABOVE: This birdbath became a plinth when its top broke. Now it supports a Chinese blue and white porcelain egg nestled comfortably in the petals of a hydrangea.

RIGHT: Subsidiary focal points can be in an area with a main focal point, but it must not be too showy. Detailing on this new house is so perfect that it, too, becomes a subsidiary focal point. Notice the carved wood, master brickwork, real stucco, copper gutters, casement windows, and its historical style in carved stone. It makes a great backdrop for a garden.

Details on your house are subsidiary focal points. Always consider color, house numbers, interior window treatments and views looking in, shutters, door hardware, light fixtures, doormat, espaliered plants, shingles, gutters and down-spouts.

ABOVE: Classic watering cans set about randomly work in any garden as subsidiary focal points.

ABOVE: Gardening is easier with a two-wheeled wheelbarrow, anyway. Use your single-wheeled wheelbarrow as a container garden.

Subsidiary Focal Points...

1. Subsidiary focal points should be discreet and not compete with the main focal point.

2. Subsidiary focal points are usually smaller items like a stone rabbit.

3. Subsidiary focal points are hidden surprises, luring the visitor to seek out points of beauty.

Both of these photos examine a subsidiary focal point.
PICTURED ABOVE: Already a focal point, this informal pond and waterfall have been splashed with a drop of red. With all green foliage, red, golden yellow, white or orange will be showiest. Burgundies and blues will recede and disappear.
OPPOSITE: Statuary heads have been used as artwork for centuries and this head is particularly nice. Depending on plantings and presentation, this head can be either a main focal point or a subsidiary focal point. With the pot in the background this head might be better as a subsidiary focal point if it were lowered 7″-8″.

Design Challenges

*I don't pull into my driveway,
I pull into my garden.*

There are things you may not be able to remove or change about your garden. When reality isn't acceptable, think illusion.

A Problem of Scale

A small back garden with a large, substantial house presented a great design challenge. Not only was the back garden small it was in front of the entrance to the neighborhood golf course. Previous owners planted extensive hedges of Leyland Cypress, which the current owners wanted to keep. Hedges hid the golf course traffic but made the tiny backyard feel oppressive. Solution, prune a 6´ x 3´ opening between two Leyland Cypresses and place an interesting wood gate with custom hardware in that space. A meandering flagstone path to the gate creates the illusion that the garden has another room and more depth. Instead of a solid wall of greenery an opening invites you to follow the path and explore.

A small garden room with a path can appear larger if the path starts wide and narrows slightly toward a focal point of diminutive size. A smaller focal point will recede.

Wall Expanses

Another illusion can be similarly created on broad expanses of your home. The sides of your home might be nothing more than a plain wall and perhaps an air-conditioner or two. Place a pair of French doors with mirrors against the wall. Add a pathway to the doors and a pot on each side.

Entryways are always focal points

Entryways are an exception to the rule of one focal point per area. A garden room can have many entryways or just one. I have yet to tire of seeing birds dashing about my garden with their flyways being my paths and entryways.

DRAWING RIGHT: A long expanse at this house now has a new entryway, all faux--boring no more. This can also be done along a boring expanse of fence. Place mirrors in old doors to give the illusion of reality. No need to literally install the mirrors, glue them on with a product called "mirror mastic." The same idea is done with old windows, too.

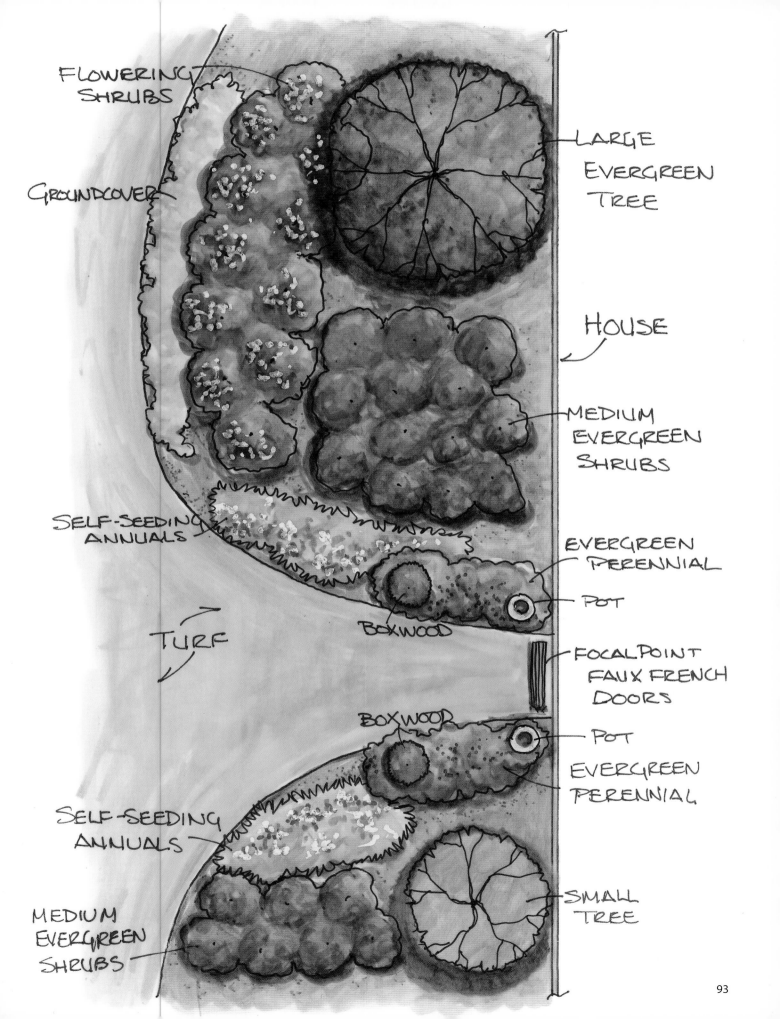

FLOWERING
SHRUBS

GROUNDCOVER

LARGE
EVERGREEN
TREE

HOUSE

MEDIUM
EVERGREEN
SHRUBS

SELF-SEEDING
ANNUALS

EVERGREEN
PERENNIAL

POT

BOXWOOD

TURF

FOCAL POINT
FAUX FRENCH
DOORS

BOXWOOD

POT

SELF-SEEDING
ANNUALS

EVERGREEN
PERENNIAL

SMALL
TREE

MEDIUM
EVERGREEN
SHRUBS

"Do not think it wasted time to submit yourself to any influence which may bring upon you any noble feeling."

J. Ruskin

ABOVE: No, this young girl statue isn't ugly but the material she's made of, cheap resin, won't benefit a garden. Real world budgets, life of the bourgeois, do make us settle for less than what we desire. Small leafed evergreen vines covering most of a cheap focal point can save it from disgrace. The same thing can be done with a focal point you don't like but which was given to you by a loved one--grow a vine on it.

RIGHT: This old neighborhood entry marker had become an eyesore through the years--so much so that the neighborhood banded together and raised funds to have it refurbished. After decades of being an eyesore it is now hard to imagine those years ever existed.

Maintenance

The worst offender to any garden is poor maintenance. Grass growing into beds can easily be remedied and make all the difference in the world to the look of the bed. Weeds growing among your blooms greatly diminish the beauty of the plant. While you are walking through your garden each evening to talk to and admire your plants, pull up those offenders. A little time for maintenance goes a long way. Remove dead plants or branches and your garden will continually look fresh and cared for. Replenish mulch; this not only improves the look of your garden but will help keep down those offending ugly weeds.

Birdfeeders

Birdfeeders can be an eyesore. Mine are quite unattractive. There is no good way to keep these looking clean and neat. However, they are the exception to what I'll allow in gardens as an ugly focal point. But several birding books and binoculars upstairs and downstairs bear witness to the pleasure gained.

LEFT & ABOVE: All gardeners should have a work area for tools, potting table, compost, and other miscellaneous goods. The work area should be readily accessible. Inherently a garden work area is junky. Don't think that way anymore. Instead think, "My work area will be so beautiful and functional it's going to be on the cover of a garden book." This garden shed and work area would be welcome in most gardens. Look closely at the compost pile, left, it's really a compost bed.

Design Offenders...

At the top of my "ugly list" is a pink stucco house with Georgia red clay splashed entirely around its base. Mulch will remedy this. Others on my list are:

1. Brick edging with holes in the bricks showing.

2. Black plastic edging.

3. A house with beautiful brick or stone using cinder blocks for retaining walls.

4. A front door mat that wore out several years ago and was too small to begin with.

5. Cheap concrete statuary, color untreated.

6. Light fixtures by the front door that are improperly scaled, typically too big, and made of pock-marked cheap brass.

RIGHT & FAR RIGHT: Gardens have secrets in pictures and video--they hold back some facts. So touring gardens is still the best way to understand how to design and work a garden. If you only saw the photo far right you would never know what it took to keep this focal point level. Garden photography can give an illusion of gardening that's far from the reality. Unfortunately, the reverse is true. Many gardens are beautiful beyond what a camera or video can capture.

Points of Illusion...

1. Create depth in an evergreen hedge by placing a six foot wooden gate in it and a flagstone path leading to it.

2. Long plain walls of your home can become charming with the addition of faux French doors, a pathway, and pair of urns.

3. Entryways are always focal points and an exception to the rule of one focal point per area.

4. A small garden room with a path can appear larger if the path starts wide and narrows slightly toward a focal point of diminutive size.

DRAWING OPPOSITE: A tiny backyard with an overwhelming hedge, blocking traffic views and noises, gave a closed-in feeling. Creating a pathway to a faux gate gives the illusion of another garden room beyond.

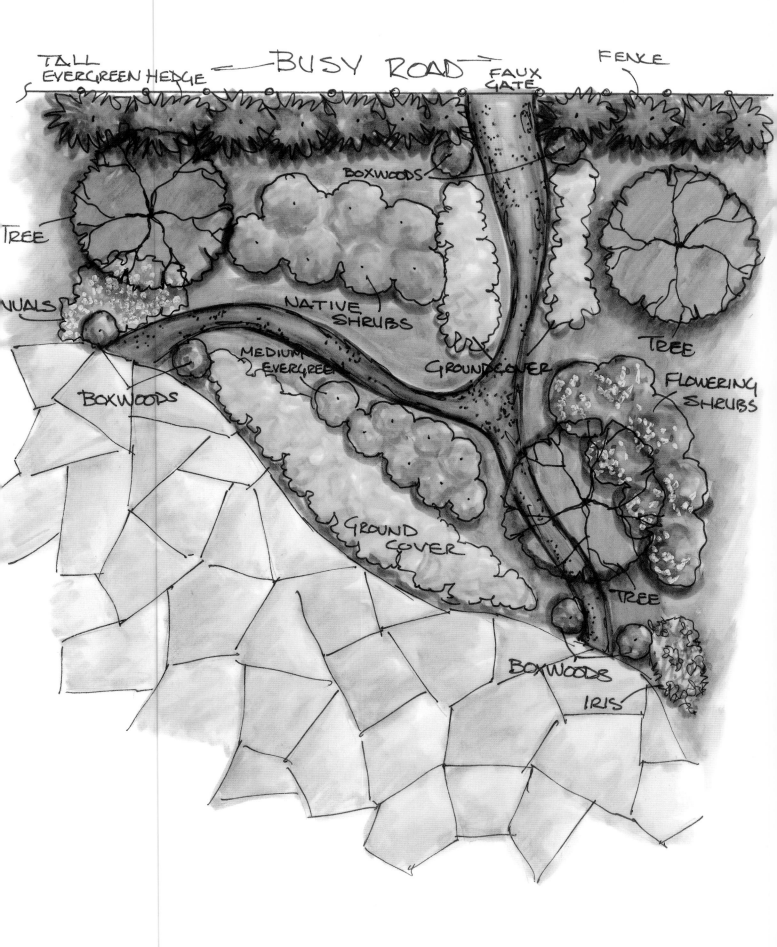

TALL
EVERGREEN HEDGE ← BUSY ROAD → FAUX FENCE
GATE

BOXWOODS

TREE

NATIVE
SHRUBS

NUALS GROUNDCOVER TREE

MEDIUM
EVERGREEN FLOWERING
SHRUBS

BOXWOODS

GROUND
COVER

TREE

BOXWOODS

IRIS

101

Installing Your Focal Points

> "...you should give your love full rein and that whatever pleasure you seize today may not be there for you to seize tomorrow."
>
> Machiavelli

Placement

This is your test at the end of the course taught in this book. Successful placement of your garden focal points is the culmination of everything you learned from the ideas I have tried to convey about the design of your garden. Consider the placement carefully. You may have to place a focal point several times, in several areas of your garden before you find the perfect place. Don't be afraid to live with the placement for a few days before permanently installing the piece.

When trying to determine the placement of heavy focal points you will want to first "play pretend" by substituting a bamboo stake of the appropriate height. Place the stake where the focal point is to be and study its placement from several vantage points. Go up to your house and look back, go into your house and look out, walk across the street and peer at it from afar. Play with placement and play with it for several days or weeks, such a major decision doesn't need to be made in one afternoon. Sometimes the exact inch of a focal point's placement is imperative. Stakes are also helpful if there are two gardeners involved. Placing stakes can prevent a

lot of disagreements.

If your landscape installation is being contracted, try to be home when the focal points are placed. Contractors will always have a few questions about the work. If you're not there, they have to answer the questions themselves, and their answers might all be contrary to your vision. You will arrive home to an unhappy scene.

All focal points must be level. You will need to check your focal points yearly and level them. No matter how inconvenient, get your focal points level.

Nothing is difficult about choosing and placing focal points, except some possible logistics. There are just a lot of simple things to ponder and implement. Follow the rules for focal points, break the rules where your soul tells you to, and create the garden of your imagination. You will be amazed at the grace it will bring into your life.

ABOVE: I don't know his name but this is one cute flamingo. He is perfectly sited, able to nibble at a meal all day. If a focal point indicates it should interact with your landscape, you should facilitate the relationship.

EVERGREEN SHRUB

FLAMINGO
FOCAL POINT
PERFECTLY
PLACED
"JUST LET
IT TOUCH"

GROUNDCOVER

ABOVE: Visualizing the landscaped flamingo as a line drawing.

I travel farthest in my garden.

Combining the Organic & Inorganic

I have a rule for inorganic focal points, whether store bought or well won from "dumpster diving."* The rule is: "Just let it touch." If your focal point is not a plant, let some foliage just touch the edges of it and art is created. If your plantings with the focal point are new, the inorganic focal point might have to be moved inches yearly as the plantings grow so that it is not engulfed. Opera is an intensification of reality and that perfectly describes a beautiful garden. Foliage "just touching" a focal point intensifies its impact.

Focal points that are made of less than desirable materials can become wonderful when armored with a coat of a tiny creeping evergreen vine such as Ivy "Duck Foot." If a bench is placed near some foliage that is "just touching," perhaps you can pull a few branches through the slats and instantly soften its presence. Many times I've been hired to design in a garden that didn't need a whole garden design but rather "garden styling." It's fun to enter a garden lacking in impact and remove some focal points, shift those that remain, and make sure any that can "just touch" some foliage do so.

It's most difficult to design and style your own garden. Practice by mentally designing and styling your friends' and neighbors' gardens.

* "Dumpster diving" is a generic term. It includes actual dumpsters but also stopping at rubbish piles on garbage day, scavenging dilapidated home sites, or poking through a pile at the welder's atelier.

Using a Plinth

A plinth is simply put--a base. In classical architecture it is the lowest member of a column or pedestal. It can be a block or a slab of material that is meant to raise an item.

Many times a focal point is perfect in every way but height. This problem is easily solved by raising it to the proper height with a plinth. Plinths can be purchased or made from what's at hand like leftover bricks or stones. My favorite plinth is made of large, field gathered quartz stones stacked one atop the other, culminating with a pot.

ABOVE: This rotted gate cannot be repaired but it hasn't retired. It carries a lady's face carved in cast stone. Gate and face together make art. Imagine this gardener's countenance when her thought processes threw together: gate, face, woods, tree, groundcover. Maybe you already have the makings of artistic focal points but inspiration about putting them together hasn't arrived yet.

ABOVE: Maybe this watering can was found in a shed or purchased at a garage sale with a hole in the bottom for $1. The origin doesn't matter when the lines and color are this good. Notice that foliage just grazes its edges, using the rule of "just let it touch."

Art From Found Objects

A garden mentor of mine, who grew up on a farm in upstate New York in the early part of the last century, taught me "It's what we do with what we have." She lived that motto in all her affairs. Her artistry took the form of interior design, cooking, weaving, collage and gardening. Her endeavors displayed artistic simplicity and originality. In addition to asking, "Is this so wonderful it will be fought over at my estate sale?" include her motto: "It's what we do with what we have." By mixing what you already have with purchased items and plants, you can create a garden of exception and wonder.

ABOVE: This spray of old garden tools was copied from an antique French toile print. Hanging them on the wall, with urns of ivy on an iron and glass hall table, was inspired by interior decorating. It's classic, whimsical, and low maintenance.

RIGHT: Here is bog garden perfection. The browning of the bog plant foliage matches exactly the rust on the tub. Would you ever imagine planting a bog garden in an old tub? This gardener got the pun of water loving plants in a water loving container. Whimsy, like this bog garden, usually works for focal points. (Cute focal points typically don't work. It's not good to make people wonder "what were they thinking?")

ABOVE: A simple stone lets you know, "yes, you're on the right path." This focal point beckons visitors and moves them into the garden.

Always Refining

You don't work in your garden, you refine your garden. Gardens change by the moment. You change, too. What you find attractive today may be unacceptable to you in one month, one year, one decade. You may go to bed happy with your garden and wake up feeling that a large area needs to be completely redone. It is just one of those garden events I put under the heading of "providential revelation."

But it is exciting. That's an understatement about life when your garden is undergoing a major refinement.

LEFT: This little staddle stone is now a focal point and will become more important in another season when most of the foliage dies away. Then it will be both a focal point and structure. What remains in winter is called "structure."
ABOVE: This old iron box has found a new home and a new use--art. It is no accident that foliage planted at its base matches in color. What fun this gardener will have through the years planting at the box, planting in the box, or opening its door and placing a statue of St. Francis inside to create a mini-shrine. This little focal point is so wonderful it would be fought over at anyone's estate sale.

Installing Focal Points...

1. Place focal points within foliage and "just let it touch."

2. Focal points with new plantings may need to be moved yearly until plants are mature.

3. Tacky focal points can become elegant when coated with an evergreen vine.

4. If your focal point is perfect in all detail except height, raise it on a plinth.

5. Plinths can be purchased or made of bricks, stone, or what ever is at hand.

6. "It's what we do with what we have." Mix what you already have with purchased items and your plants to create an original garden.

Gardens and houses should be intimate.

ABOVE: Woodland gardens can look beautiful with or without focal points. This woodland had the misfortune of having several diseased trees cut down. Grinding the stumps would have disrupted the garden too greatly, so they were left. What eyesores they became. Most of the stumps were covered with foliage, but this stump sprouted a new idea--a focal point. The pot not only gained a plinth, but the stump became useful instead of an eyesore.

Installing Focal Points...

7. "Play pretend" by first substituting a bamboo stake when placing your focal points.

8. Look at the bamboo stake from near the house, inside the house, across the street--all views.

9. Play with placement for several days. A decision doesn't need to be made in one afternoon.

10. Sometimes the exact inch of a focal point's placement is imperative.

11. Bamboo stakes can prevent disagreements if two gardeners are involved.

12. If using a contractor, be home when focal points are being placed.

13. All focal points must be level.

> *"It is just in the way it is done that lies the whole difference between commonplace gardening and gardening that may rightly claim to rank as a fine art."*
>
> Gertrude Jekyll

Knowing so many facets of designing my garden doesn't mean I can redesign an area by just standing there and giving it a few minutes thought. For instance, for my own focal points, I stand and sit inside looking at the outside view, getting macro ideas about where the focal point and its plants will go. My phone is off the hook during this entire process. Then I go outside into the space and sit in a chair, intuitively feeling the feng shui about the macro changes I envision. My semi-final decisions are made outside in the garden. I go back inside to finalize the decision, then outside again to set macro and micro changes on paper. One focal point recently required me to walk across the street and stand three houses away, just standing and looking--looking intently. I want that focal point to draw my eye while driving home in my car where a curve crests, finally letting me see my garden.

Placing focal points is a process like I just described. My success rate is about 97%. The 3% failures are exposed while turning theory into practice. What's good in theory or drawn on paper isn't necessarily good in three dimensional reality. My "failures" have all needed to be moved forward, backward, or higher a few feet.

An armillary sundial I acquired years ago has never been displayed in my garden. It's a great piece, real bronze, but I can't find a home for it. Searching, searching, searching, I am enjoying the anticipation of finding the perfect spot for it someday.

Focal points in my garden can quickly become "nothings"--mere plinths for the birds, butterflies, squirrels, and chipmunks that rest on them. Seeing wildlife living in my garden makes me laugh at my pretensions. I sense Mother Nature saying, "Yes, I see what you can do, now here's a little of what I can do." But it's not a competition. Victory is still there because focal points are on axes with every window and I get to see all the interaction of my focal points with Mother Nature's input.

LEFT: If you don't look closely you won't realize the hydrangea was singled out to be a focal point by planting it in a container and raising its height. Planting a couple of extra 20″ diameter containers with large shrubs can come in handy. Use them to fill in any gaps if a plant has died or you wish to add extra punch.

PAGES 118 & 119: This is today's antique garden gnome. Most of us can't remember the glory days of garden gnomes because they had already become ubiquitous jokes. Poor gnomes. Their legions were greatly diminished, so now they are appealing again. Scarcity creates desire. This gnome has found a caring home. His gardener has matched flower colors to his clothing. He spends winter vacation indoors.

What is it? A neat focal point for one thing.

Dynamic Cultural Anthropology as Focal Point

LEFT: This potager garden has an unusual trellis--an old copper light fixture. Keep looking, always be looking, and thinking how anything in a pile of junk can be used in your garden. "Dumpster diving" focal points can create unique gardens. Picasso was a junking man, making sculptures from what he found. Use only the artistic best for your garden.

ABOVE: House and garden together are telling a story here. Little to none of the original garden remains. What does remain speaks of different decades--the 1950s, 1970s, 1990s and many years of non-gardeners. The current owners are obvious gardeners because of the attention to maintenance. I look at this garden and see a focal point of history and a garden on the cusp of great change--with new owners and a new decade.

*Just
let it
touch*

LEFT: So what if you can't sit here anymore. This bench is aging better than most people--its beauty is increasing. The rule of "just let it touch" is used here with an addendum: "Make it caress." Most focal points have greater impact when foliage is gracing their edges.

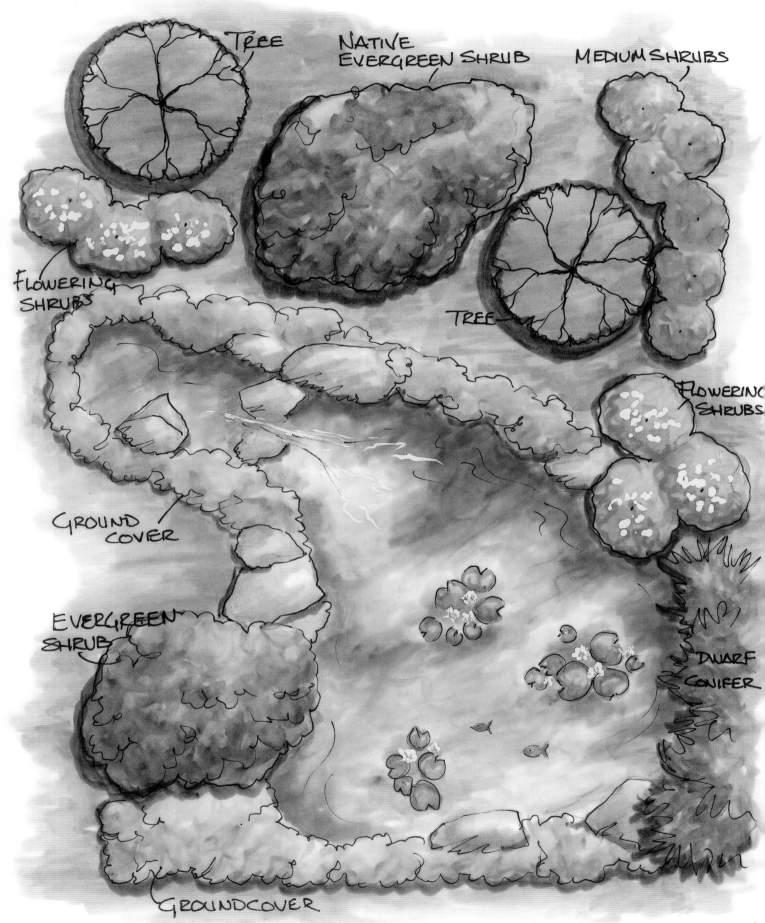

TREE

NATIVE
EVERGREEN SHRUB

MEDIUM SHRUBS

FLOWERING
SHRUBS

TREE

FLOWERING
SHRUBS

GROUND
COVER

EVERGREEN
SHRUB

DWARF
CONIFER

GROUNDCOVER

DWG 12 Shannon Lee

DRAWING OPPOSITE: Ponds are focal points until the water lilies bloom, the cherry tree blossoms, or the maples burst into color in fall. Remember to include acts of nature as focal points.
ABOVE: These are perennial water lilies. Photograph your temporary focal points. This picture makes a permanent focal point record of a water lily long gone. Photographing your garden is important because it saves, within another art form, the beauty of your garden. Make a goal to photograph areas with a focal point through four seasons. Keep doing this through the years, and what a story you will have in pictures!

Inches to Millimeters and Centimeters

Inches	MM	CM
1/8	3	.3
1/4	6	.6
3/8	10	1.0
1/2	13	1.3
5/8	16	1.6
3/4	19	1.9
7/8	22	2.2
1	25	2.5
1-1/4	32	3.2
1-1/2	38	3.8
1-3/4	44	4.4
2	51	5.1
3	76	7.6
4	102	10.2
5	127	12.7
6	152	15.2
7	178	17.8
8	203	20.3
9	229	22.9
10	254	25.4
11	279	27.9
12	305	30.5

Yards to Meters

Yards	Meters
1/8	.11
1/4	.23
3/8	.34
1/2	.46
5/8	.57
3/4	.69
7/8	.80
1	.91
2	1.83
3	2.74
4	3.66
5	4.57
6	5.49
7	6.40
8	7.32
9	8.23
10	9.14